Dhammapada

A practical guide to right living

Venerable
Sri Acharya Buddharakkhita

Reprinted by
Kong Meng San Phor Kark See Monastery

DHAMMAPADA

Reprinted by

Kong Meng San Phor Kark See Monastery

Dharma Propagation Division
Awaken Publishing and Design
88 Bright Hill Road, Singapore 574117
Tel: (65) 6849 5342
E-mail: publication@kmspks.org
Web: www.kmspks.org

Published for free distribution by
Sukhi Hotu Sdn Bhd

1-T Jalan Gottlieb
10350 Pulau Pinang, Malaysia
Tel & Fax: +6 04 229 4811
Email: shpg@sukhihotu.com

———

D9-6-1 Block D9
Dana 1 Commercial Centre
Jalan PJU 1A/46
47301 Petaling Jaya, Selangor, Malaysia
Tel & Fax: +6 03 7842 6828
Email: shpj@sukhihotu.com

———

Web: www. sukhihotu.com

The publisher gratefully acknowledges the permission
kindly given by the author to reprint this pocket edition
for free distribution.
Reprinted August 2013 – 3,000 books
Printed by Fabulous Printers Pte Ltd
Book layout and cover design by Jotika
Special credit—*Rebecca Tam, Pauline Chong & Jat Yeen*

ISBN 978-983-9382-13-6
EDHAMM-0202-0813

Published with environmental mindfulness
Printed in Singapore on eco-friendly paper made from sustainable forests

CONTENTS

PREFACE

The Dhammapada, an anthology of four hundred and twenty-three verses, compiled approximately six hundred years before Christ, belongs to the Khuddaka Nikaya ("Compact Collection") of the sacred Buddhist scripture, the Tipitaka. Handed down in the Pali language, in which the Buddha spoke, the Tipitaka (lit., "Three Baskets") has preserved the original teachings of the Enlightened One.

The Buddha enunciated his Dhamma (Teachings) in two different forms. Though distinct, they ultimately converge in the unfolding of insight into the realities of existence and the Beyond. One approach was in philosophical terms, incisive and analytical. The other took the form of discourses in simple, direct language intelligible to the masses, and often precipitated by a specific question or incident. It is from this body of material that the Dhammapada was compiled. Each verse was prompted by a particular episode, accounts of which are preserved in the Dhammapada Atthakatha, one of the commentaries on the Pali canon.

What the Gita is to Hindus, the Bible to Christendom and the Koran to Islamic people, the Dhammapada is to the Buddhist world. For the simple and unsophisticated, it is a sympathetic counsellor; for the intellectually overburdened its clear and direct teachings inspire humility and reflection; for the earnest seeker, it is a perennial source of inspiration. Insights that flashed into the heart of the Buddha have crystallized into these luminous verses of pure wisdom. As profound expressions of practical spirituality, each verse is a guideline to right living. The Buddha unambiguously pointed out that whoever earnestly practices the verses of the Dhammapada would taste the bliss of emancipation.

In preparing this volume I have had access to numerous editions and translations in various languages, including Sanskrit, Hindi, Bengali, Sinhalese, Burmese and Nepali. While consulting a number of English editions, it was observed that the renderings were often either too free and inaccurate or too pedantic. It was therefore felt that a new edition of the Dhammapada, avoiding these two extremes, would be beneficial to readers.

There are editions of the Dhammapada by noted scholars such as Max Muller and Dr. S. Radhakrishnan. However, the teachings of the Buddha inevitably suffer some distortion when presented from a non-Buddhist frame of reference. Erroneous ideas have sometimes resulted from an unfortunate selection of words in translation, and foot-notes have at times been judgmental. The present translation by a practicing follower of the Buddha is a humble effort to transmit the spirit and content as well as the language and style of the original teachings.

Where a few of the verses are conundrums

or contain analogies not immediately evident to the reader, the meanings are provided either in parenthesis or notes. For interpretation I have relied on the classic 5th century A.D. commentary by Bhadantacariya Buddhaghosa, the great Buddhist savant.

The Pali literature is a veritable storehouse of knowledge. It includes not only the Buddhist scriptures but also commentarial literature and independent treatises containing rich material on the science of mind, medicine, the history and geography of ancient India and surrounding countries, literature, poetics, prosody, the prevalent technology and civics, sports, martial arts, etc. Students of psychology, sociology, anthropology and cosmology will find the Pali literature a mine of source-material for their disciplines. It is to be noted that much of Asia, particularly Burma, Cambodia, Sri Lanka, Thailand and Vietnam, built distinctive civilizations inspired by the Pali tradition.

I am grateful to Upasika Karunamma, an esteemed American pupil, for the most devoted service and help in going through the manuscript and suggesting improvements. Without her unreserved help, this edition would never have materialized.

In grateful memory of my teachers, parents and relatives, departed and living, I humbly make an offering of the Punya (spiritual merit) accruing from the effort of preparing this work. May they attain Nibbana!

May all beings be happy!

ACHARYA BUDDHARAKKHITA
Maha Bodhi Ashram, Bangalore, India
16th October 1986

INTRODUCTION

From ancient times to the present, the Dhamma-pada has been regarded as the most succinct expression of the Buddha's teaching. In the countries following Theravada Buddhism, it is a guidebook for everyday life. Even withdrawn contemplatives must possess a copy of the book. Yet the admiration of Dhammapada has not been confined to followers of Buddhism. Wherever it has become known its aphoristic wisdom and stirring message have won veneration of all.

The son of a king, the Buddha, was born in sixth century B.C. His name was Siddhattha and family name Gotama (Sanskrit: Siddhartha Gautama). Groomed to be heir to the throne, he encountered disturbing facts of suffering and lost all interest in the pleasures and privileges of rulership. One night, in his twenty-ninth year, he left home and became an ascetic, resolved to find the way to deliverance from suffering. For six years he experimented with different religious systems, subjected himself to severe austerities, but found that these practices did not bring him any closer to his goal. Finally, in his thirty-fifth year, sitting in deep meditation beneath the Bodhi tree at Gaya, he attained Supreme Enlightenment and become the Buddha. Thereafter, for forty-five years, he travelled throughout India, proclaiming the truths he had discovered and founding an order of monks and nuns to carry on his message. At the age of eighty, after a long and fruitful life, he passed away peacefully in Kusinara, surrounded by a large number of disciples.

To his followers, the Buddha is neither a god, a divine incarnation, nor a prophet bearing a message of divine revelation, but one who has reached the highest spiritual attainment, Supreme Enlightenment (Bodhi). He is a world teacher who, out of compassion, points out the way to Nibbana,

(Sanskrit: Nirvana), final release from suffering. His teaching, known as the Dhamma, offers a body of instructions explaining the true nature of existence and showing the path that leads to liberation. Free from all dogmas and inscrutable claims to authority, the Dhamma is founded upon Buddha's own realization of reality, and leads one who practices it to that excellence.

In its twenty-six chapters, Dhammapada spans multiple aspects of the Buddha's teaching, offering a variety of standpoints from which to gain a glimpse into the heart of Dhamma-Truth. The inspirational verses on the fundamentals of the Dhamma are meant to be used as a basis for personal edification and instruction. As water, though one in essence, assumes different shapes due to the vessels into which it is poured, so the Dhamma of liberation takes on different forms in response to the needs of the beings to be taught. This diversity is evident in the verses of Dhammapada.

The Buddha's teachings found in the Dhamma-pada apparently are designed to meet three primary aims: human welfare here and now, a favourable rebirth in the next life, and the attainment of the ultimate good. The last aim is twofold: path and fruit.

The first aim is concerned with establishing wellbeing and happiness in the immediately visible sphere of concrete human relations. This level shows man the way to live at peace with himself and his fellow men, to fulfill his family and social responsibilities, and to restrain conflict and violence which infect the individual, society, and the world. The guidelines here are basic ethical injunctions proposed by most world religions, but in the Buddha's teaching they are freed from theistic moorings and grounded upon two directly verifiable foundations: concern for one's own integrity and happiness and welfare of others. For instance, one should avoid all evil, cultivate the good and cleanse one's mind (183). Other verses provide more specific directives. One should avoid irritability in deed, word and thought and exercise self-control (231-234), and practice the five precepts, which teach abstinence from destroying life, from stealing, from committing adultery, from speaking lies and from taking intoxicants, treat all beings with kindness and compassion, live honestly and righteously. Instead of finding others' faults one should examine one's own faults, make a continual effort to remove impurities just as a silversmith purifies silver (50, 239). There is no need to despair for past evil; one who abandons the evil for the good "illuminates this world like the moon freed from clouds (173)."

The Buddha's teaching reveals moral justice in an impersonal universal law, the law of Kamma, which reigns over all sentient existence. Kamma means action springing from intention, as bodily deed, speech, and thought. Unwholesome kamma is action rooted in mental states of greed, hatred and delusion; and wholesome kamma, action rooted in mental states of generosity or detachment, goodwill and understanding. The willed actions may fade from memory but they leave subtle imprints on the mind, seeds with the potential to come to fruition. The objective field in which the seeds of kamma ripen is the process of rebirths called samsara.

Life is not an isolated occurrence beginning with birth and ending in death. Each single lifespan is part of series of lives having no discoverable beginning in time and continuing on as long as the desire for existence stands intact. Rebirth can take place in various realms. There are not only the familiar realms of human beings and animals, but ranged above we meet heavenly worlds of greater happiness, beauty and power and ranged below infernal worlds of extreme suffering. The cause for rebirth is kamma. Kamma determines the sphere into which rebirth takes place, wholesome actions bringing rebirth in higher forms, unwholesome actions rebirth in lower forms. After yielding rebirth, kamma continues to operate, governing the endowments and circumstances.

The second level of teaching found in the Dhammapada is to follow this ethical law leading upwards—to inner development, to higher rebirths and to richer experiences of happiness and joy. However, all states of existence in samsara, even the lofty celestial abodes, are lacking in genuine worth: for they are all inherently impermanent, without any lasting substance, and thus, for those who cling to them, potential bases for suffering. The disciple of mature faculties, does not long even for rebirth among the gods. Having understood the intrinsic inadequacy of all conditioned things, his only aspiration is Nibbana, the unconditioned state where there is no more birth, ageing and death, and no more suffering.

The third level of teaching found in the Dhammapada emerges out of this aspiration for final deliverance. The Four Noble Truths provide the frame work for this aim. The first truth concerns various forms of suffering, existence itself being impermanent and substanceless, is intrinsically unsatisfactory. The second truth is craving for pleasure and existence which drives us through the round of rebirths, bringing in its trail suffering. The third truth declares that the destruction of craving issues in release from suffering, and the fourth prescribes the means to gain release, the Noble Eightfold Path: right understanding, right thought, right speech, right action, right livelihood, right effort, right mindfulness, and right concentration (Chapter 20).

The Noble Eightfold Path is arranged into three groups of training: Moral discipline, concentration and wisdom. By the training in morality, the coarse forms of mental defilements are kept under control. By the training in concentration, the mind is made calm, pure and unified. The training in wisdom climaxes in the deliverance of mind.

The practice of the path in all three stages is feasible for people in any walk of life. The Buddha taught it to lay people as well as to monks, and many of his lay followers reached high stages of attainment. However, application to the development of the path becomes most fruitful for those who have relinquished all other concerns in order to devote themselves wholeheartedly to spiritual training, to living the 'holy life' (brahmacariya). Thus the Buddha established the Sangha, the order of monks and nuns, as the special field for those ready to dedicate their lives to the practice of his path, and in the Dhammapada the call to the monastic life resounds throughout.

The Dhammapada acclaims those who have reached the goal. At the first, called "Stream-entry" the disciple gains his first glimpse of "The Deathless", and enters irreversibly upon the path to liberation. This achievement alone, the Dhammapada declares, is greater than lordship over all the worlds (178). Following Stream-entry come two further stages which weaken and eradicate still more defilements and bring the goal increasingly closer to view. One is called the stage of Once-returner, the other the stage of non-returner. The fourth and final stage is that of the Arahat, the Perfected One, the fully accomplished sage who has completed the development of the path, eradicated all defilements and freed himself from the cycle of rebirths. This is the ideal figure of the Dhammapada. Extolled in Chapter 7 the Arahat serves as a living demonstration of the truth of the Dhamma.

The Arahat ideal reaches its optimal exemplification in the Buddha, the promulgator and master of the entire teaching. It was the Buddha who, without any aid or guidance, rediscovered the ancient path to deliverance and taught it to countless others. His arising in the world provides the precious opportunity to hear and practice the excellent Dhamma (182, 194). He is the giver of refuge (190, 192), the Supreme Teacher who depends on nothing but his own self-evolved wisdom (353).

BHIKKHU BODHI
Forest Hermitage, Kandy.

Namo Tassa Bhagavato Arahato Sammasambuddhassa

**Homage to Him, the Blessed One, the Perfected One,
the Supremely Enlightened One**

Dhammapada
A practical guide to right living

Chapter 1

THE PAIRS

1

Mind precedes all mental states.
Mind is their chief;
they are all mind-wrought.
If with an impure mind
a person speaks or acts,
suffering follows him like the wheel
that follows the foot of the ox.

2

Mind precedes all mental states.
Mind is their chief;
they are all mind-wrought.
If with a pure mind
a person speaks or acts,
happiness follows him
like his never-departing shadow.

3

"He abused me,
he struck me,
he overpowered me,
he robbed me."
Those who harbour such thoughts
do not still their hatred.

4

"He abused me,
he struck me,
he overpowered me,
he robbed me."
Those who do not harbour such thoughts
still their hatred.

5

Hatred is never appeased
by hatred in this world.
By non-hatred alone
is hatred appeased.
This is a Law Eternal.[1]

6

There are those
who do not realize
that one day we all must die.
But those who do realize this
settle their quarrels.

7

Just as a storm
throws down a weak tree,
so does Mara[2] overpower the man
who lives for the pursuit of pleasures,
who is uncontrolled in his senses,
immoderate in eating,
indolent and dissipated.

8

Just as a storm
cannot prevail against a rocky mountain,
so Mara can never overpower
the man who lives meditating
on the impurities, who is controlled
in his senses, moderate in eating,
and filled with faith and earnest effort.[3]

9

Whoever being depraved,
devoid of self-control
and truthfulness
should don the monk's yellow robe,
he surely is not worthy of the robe.

10

But whoever is purged of depravity,
well-established in virtues
and filled with self-control
and truthfulness,
he indeed is worthy of the yellow robe.

11
Those who mistake
the unessential to be essential
and the essential to be unessential,
dwelling in wrong thoughts,
never arrive at the essential.

12
Those who know
the essential to be essential
and the unessential to be unessential,
dwelling in right thoughts,
do arrive at the essential.

13

Just as rain
breaks through
an ill-thatched house,
so passion penetrates
an undeveloped mind.

14

Just as rain
does not break through
a well-thatched house,
so passion never penetrates
a well-developed mind.

15

The evil-doer
grieves here and hereafter;
he grieves in both the worlds.
He laments and is afflicted,
recollecting his own impure deeds.

16

The doer of good
rejoices here and hereafter;
he rejoices in both the worlds.
He rejoices and exults,
recollecting his own pure deeds.

17
The evil-doer
suffers here and hereafter;
he suffers in both the worlds.
The thought, "Evil have I done,"
torments him, and he suffers
even more when gone to realms of woe.[4]

18
The doer of good
delights here and hereafter;
he delights in both the worlds.
The thought, "Good have I done,"
delights him, and he delights
even more when gone to realms of bliss.[5]

19
Much though he recites
the sacred texts,
but acts not accordingly,
that heedless man
is like a cowherd
who only counts the cows of others —
he does not partake
of the blessings of a holy life.

20

Little though
he recites the sacred texts,
but puts the Teaching
into practice,
forsaking lust, hatred and delusion,
with true wisdom
and emancipated mind
clinging to nothing
of this or any other world –
he indeed partakes
of the blessings of a holy life.

Chapter 2

HEEDFULNESS

21

Heedfulness is the path to the Deathless.
Heedlessness is the path to death.
The heedful die not.
The heedless are as if dead already.[6]

22

Clearly understanding
this excellence of heedfulness,
the wise exult therein and enjoy the resort
of the Noble Ones.[7]

23

The wise ones, ever meditative
and steadfastly persevering,
alone experience Nibbana,
the incomparable freedom
from bondage.

24

Ever grows the glory of him
who is energetic, mindful
and pure in conduct,
discerning and self-controlled,
righteous and heedful.

25

By effort and heedfulness,
discipline and self-mastery,
let the wise one make for himself
an island which no flood can overwhelm.

26

The foolish and ignorant
indulge in heedlessness,
but the wise one keeps his heedfulness
as his best treasure.

27
Do not give way to heedlessness.
Do not indulge in sensual pleasures.
Only the heedful and meditative
attain great happiness.

28
Just as one upon the summit
of a mountain
beholds the groundings,
even so when the wise man
casts away heedlessness
by heedfulness
and ascends
the high tower of wisdom,
this sorrowless sage beholds
the sorrowing and foolish
multitude.

29

Heedful among the heedless,
wide-awake among the sleepy,
the wise man advances
like a swift horse
leaving behind a weak jade.

30

By heedfulness did Indra*
become the overlord of the gods.
Heedfulness is ever praised,
and heedlessness ever despised.

---

*Ruler of the gods in ancient Indian Mythology.

31

The monk who delights
in heedfulness
and looks with fear at heedlessness
advances like fire,
burning all fetters small and large.

32

The monk who delights
in heedfulness
and looks with fear at heedlessness
will not fall.
He is close to Nibbana.

Chapter 3

THE MIND

33

Just as a fletcher straightens
an arrow shaft,
even so the discerning man
straightens his mind –
so fickle and unsteady,
so difficult to guard and control.

34

As a fish when pulled out of water
and cast on land
throbs and quivers,
even so is this mind agitated.
Hence should one abandon
the realm of Mara.

35

Wonderful, indeed,
it is to subdue the mind,
so difficult to subdue, ever swift,
and seizing whatever it desires.
A tamed mind brings happiness.

36

Let the discerning man
guard the mind,
so difficult to detect and extremely subtle,
seizing whatever it desires.
A guarded mind brings happiness.

37
Dwelling in the cave[8] (of the heart),
the mind, without form,
wanders far and alone.
Those who subdue this mind
are liberated from the bonds of Mara.

38
Wisdom never becomes perfect
in one whose mind is not steadfast,
who knows not the Good Teaching
and whose faith wavers.

39

There is no fear for an awakened one,
whose mind is not sodden
(by lust)
nor afflicted
(by hate),
and who has gone beyond
both merit and demerit.[9]

40
Realizing that this body
is as fragile as a clay pot,
and fortifying this mind
like
a well-fortified city,
fight out Mara
with the sword of wisdom.
Then, guarding the conquest,
remain unattached.

41
Ere long, alas!
This body will lie upon the earth,
unheeded and lifeless,
like a useless log.

42
Whatever harm an enemy
may do to an enemy,
or a hater to a hater,
an ill-directed mind
inflicts on oneself a greater harm.

43

Neither mother, father,
nor any other relative
can do one greater good
than one's own well-directed mind.

Chapter 4

FLOWERS

44

Who shall overcome this earth,
this realm of Yama
and this sphere of men and gods?
Who shall bring to perfection
the well-taught path of wisdom
as an expert garland-maker
would his floral design?[10]

45

A striver-on-the-path
shall overcome this earth,
this realm of Yama
and this sphere of men and gods.
The striver-on-the-path
shall bring to perfection
the well-taught path of wisdom,
as an expert garland-maker would
his floral design.[11]

46

Realizing that this body is like froth,
penetrating its mirage-like nature,
and plucking out Mara's
flower-tipped arrows of sensuality,
go beyond sight of the King of Death!

47

As a mighty flood
sweeps away the sleeping village,
so death carries away the person
of distracted mind
who only plucks the flowers (of pleasure).

48

The Destroyer
brings under his sway
the person of distracted mind who,
insatiate in sense desires,
only plucks the flowers (of pleasure).

49

As a bee gathers honey
from the flower without injuring
its colour or fragrance,
even so the sage goes on his alms-round
in the village.[12]

50

Let none find fault with others;
let none see the omissions
and commissions of others.
But let one see one's own acts,
done and undone.

51

Like a beautiful flower
full of colour but without fragrance,
even so,
fruitless are the fair words
of one who does not practise them.

52

Like a beautiflul flower of colour
and also fragrant,
even so,
fruitful are the fair words
of one who practises them.

53

As from a great heap of flowers
many garlands can be made,
even so should many good deeds
be done by one born a mortal.

54
Not the sweet smell of flowers,
not even the fragrance of sandal,
tagara or jasmine
blows against the wind.
But the fragrance of the virtuous
blows against the wind.
Truly, the virtuous man
pervades all directions
with the fragrance of his virtue.[13]

55

Of all the fragrances—
sandal, tagara, blue lotus and jasmine—
the fragrance of virtue
is by far the sweetest.

56

Faint is the fragrance
of tagara and sandal,
but excellent is the fragrance
of the virtuous,
wafting even amongst the gods.

57

Mara never finds the path
of the truly virtuous,
who abide in heedfulness
and are freed by perfect knowledge.

58-59

Upon a heap of rubbish
in the road-side ditch blooms a lotus,
fragrant and pleasing.
Even so, on the rubbish heap
of blinded mortals the disciple
of the Supremely Enlightened One shines
resplendent in wisdom.

Chapter 5

THE FOOLS

60
Long is the night to the sleepless;
long is the league to the weary.
Long is worldly existence to fools
who know not the Sublime Truth.

61
Should a seeker not find
a companion who is better or equal,
let him resolutely pursue a solitary course;
there is no fellowship with the fool.

62

The fool worries, thinking,
"I have sons, I have wealth."
Indeed, when he himself is not his own,
whence are sons, whence is wealth?

63

A fool who knows his foolishness
is wise at least to that extent,
but a fool who thinks himself wise
is called a fool indeed.

64

Though all his life a fool associates
with a wise man,
he no more comprehends
the Truth
than a spoon tastes the flavour of the soup.

65

Though only for a moment
a discerning person associates
with a wise man,
quickly he comprehends the Truth,
just as the tongue tastes
the flavour of the soup.

66
Fools of little wit are enemies
unto themselves as they move about
doing evil deeds,
the fruits of which are bitter.

67
Ill done is that action doing
which one repents later,
and the fruit of which one,
weeping, reaps with tears.

68

Well done is that action doing
which one repents not later,
and the fruit of which one reaps
with delight and happiness.

69

So long as an evil deed has not ripened,
the fool thinks it as sweet as honey.
But when the evil deed ripens,
the fool comes to grief.[14]

70

Month after month
a fool may eat his food
with the tip of a blade of grass,
but he still is not worth
a sixteenth part
of those who have comprehended
the Truth.

71

Truly, an evil deed committed
does not immediately bear fruit,
like milk that does not
turn sour all at once.
But smouldering, it follows the fool
like fire covered by ashes.

72
To his own ruin
the fool gains knowledge,
for it cleaves his head and
destroys his innate goodness.

73
The fool seeks undeserved reputation,
precedence among monks,
authority over monasteries,
and honour among householders.

74
"Let both laymen and monks
think that it was done by me.
In every work, great and small,
let them follow me"
—such is the ambition of the fool;
thus his desire and pride increase.

75
One is the quest for worldly gain,
and quite another is the path to Nibbana.
Clearly understanding this,
let not the monk,
the disciple of the Buddha,
be carried away by worldly acclaim,
but develop detachment instead.

Chapter 6

THE WISE MAN

76
Should one find a man
who points out faults and who reproves,
let him follow
such a wise and sagacious person
as one would a guide to hidden treasure.
It is always better,
and never worse,
to cultivate such an association.

77
Let him admonish,
instruct and shield one from wrong;
he, indeed,
is dear to the good
and detestable to the evil.

78
Do not associate
with evil companions;
do not seek the fellowship of the vile.
Associate with good friends;
seek the fellowship of noble men.

79

He who drinks deep
the Dhamma
lives happily
with a tranquil mind.
The wise man ever delights
in the Dhamma made known
by the Noble One (the Buddha).

80

Irrigators regulate the waters;
fletchers straighten the arrow shaft;
carpenters shape the wood;
the wise control themselves.

81

Just as a solid rock
is not shaken by the storm,
even so the wise are not affected
by praise or blame.

82

On hearing the Teachings,
the wise become perfectly purified,
like a lake deep,
clear and still.

83
The good renounce
(attachment for) everything.
The virtuous
do not prattle
with a yearning for pleasures.
The wise
show no elation or depression
when touched
by happiness or sorrow.

84

He is indeed virtuous,
wise and righteous
who neither for his own sake
nor for the sake of another
(does any wrong),
who does not crave for sons,
wealth or kingdom,
and does not desire
success by unjust means.

85
Few among men
are those
who cross to the farther shore.
The rest, the bulk of men,
only run up and down the hither bank.

86
But those who act
according
to the perfectly taught Dhamma
will cross the realm of Death,
so difficult to cross.

87-88
Abandoning the dark way,
let the wise man cultivate
the bright path.
Having gone from home
to homelessness,
let him yearn for that delight
in detachment,
so difficult to enjoy.
Giving up sensual pleasures,
with no attachment,
let the wise man cleanse
himself of defilements of the mind.

89
Those whose minds
have reached
full excellence
in the factors of enlightenment,
who, having renounced
acquisitiveness,
rejoice in not clinging to things—
rid of cankers,
glowing with wisdom,
they have attained Nibbana
in this very life.[15]

Chapter 7

THE PERFECTED ONE

90

The fever of passion
exists not for him
who has completed the journey,
who is sorrowless and wholly set free,
and has broken all ties.[16]

91

The mindful ones exert themselves.
They are not attached
to any home;
like swans that abandon the lake,
they leave
home after home behind.

92

Those who do not accumulate
and are wise regarding food,
whose object is the Void,
the Unconditioned Freedom—
their track cannot be traced,
like that of birds in the air.[17]

93

He whose cankers
are destroyed
and who is not attached to food,
whose object is the Void,
the Unconditioned Freedom—
his path cannot be traced,
like that of birds in the air.

94

Even the gods hold dear
the wise one,
whose senses are subdued,
like horses well trained
by a charioteer,
whose pride is destroyed
and who is free from the cankers.

95

There is no more worldly existence
for the wise one,
who, like the earth,
resents nothing,
who is as firm as a high pillar
and as pure as a deep pool
free from mud.

96

Calm is his thought,
calm his speech and calm his deed,
who, truly knowing,
is wholly freed,
perfectly tranquil and wise.

97
The man
who is without blind faith,
who knows the Uncreate,
who has severed all links,
destroyed all causes
(for karma, good and evil),
and thrown out all desires—
he, truly,
is the most excellent of men.

98
Inspiring, indeed,
is that place where Arahats dwell,
be it a village, a forest,
a vale or a hill.

99
Inspiring are the forests
in which worldlings find no pleasure.
There the passionless will rejoice,
for they seek no sensual pleasures.

Chapter 8

THE THOUSANDS

100

Better than
a thousand useless words
is one useful word,
hearing which
one attains peace.

101

Better than
a thousand useless verses
is one useful verse,
hearing which
one attains peace.

102
Better than
reciting a hundred meaningless verses
is the reciting
of one verse of Dhamma,
hearing which one attains peace.

103
Though one may conquer
a thousand times a thousand men in battle,
yet he indeed is the noblest victor
who conquers himself.

104-105

Self-conquest
is far better than
the conquest of others.
Not even a god, an angel,
Mara or Brahma
can turn into defeat
the victory of such a person
who is self-subdued
and ever restrained in conduct.[18]

106
Though month after month
for a hundred years
one should offer sacrifices
by the thousands,
yet if only for a moment
one should worship
those of perfected minds
that honour is indeed better
than a century of sacrifice.

107
Though for a hundred years
one should tend
the sacrificial fire in the forest,
yet if only for a moment
one should worship
those of perfected minds
that worship is indeed better
than a century of sacrifice.

108

Whatever gifts and oblations
one seeking merit
might offer in this world
for a whole year,
all that is not worth
one fourth of the merit
gained by revering the Upright Ones,
which is truly excellent.

109
To one ever eager
to revere and serve the elders,
these four blessings accrue:
long life and beauty,
happiness and power.

110
Better it is to live one day
virtuous and meditative
than to live a hundred years
immoral and uncontrolled.

111

Better it is to live
one day wise and meditative
than to live a hundred years
foolish and uncontrolled.

112

Better it is to live
one day strenuous and resolute
than to live a hundred years
sluggish and dissipated.

113
Better it is to live
one day seeing the rise and fall of things
than to live a hundred years
without ever seeing
the rise and fall of things.

114

Better it is to live one day
seeing the Deathless
than to live a hundred years
without ever seeing
the Deathless.

115

Better it is to live one day
seeing the Supreme Truth
than to live a hundred years
without ever seeing
the Supreme Truth.

Chapter 9

EVIL

116
Hasten to do good;
restrain your mind from evil.
He who is slow in doing good,
his mind delights in evil.

117
Should a person commit evil,
let him not do it again and again.
Let him not find pleasure therein,
for painful is the accumulation of evil.

118

Should a person do good,
let him do it again and again.
Let him find pleasure therein,
for blissful is the accumulation of good.

119

It may be well with the evil-doer
as long as the evil ripens not.
But when it does ripen,
then the evil-doer sees
(the painful results of) his evil deeds.

120

It may be ill with the doer of good
as long as the good ripens not.
But when it does ripen,
then the doer of good sees
(the pleasant results of) his good deeds.

121

Think not lightly of evil, saying,
"It will not come to me."
Drop by drop is the water pot filled.
Likewise, the fool,
gathering it little by little,
fills himself with evil.

122

Think not lightly of good, saying,
"It will not come to me."
Drop by drop is the water pot filled.
Likewise, the wise man,
gathering it little by little,
fills himself with good.

123

Just as a trader
with a small escort
and great wealth would avoid
a perilous route,
or just as one desiring to live
avoids poison,
even so should one shun evil.

124

If on the hand there is no wound,
one may carry even poison in it.
Poison does not affect one
who is free from wounds.
For him who does no evil, there is no ill.

125

Like fine dust thrown against the wind,
evil falls back upon that fool
who offends an inoffensive,
pure and guiltless man.

126

Some are born in the womb;
the wicked are born in hell;
the devout go to heaven;
the stainless pass into Nibbana.

127

Neither in the sky nor in mid-ocean,
nor by entering into mountain clefts,
nowhere in the world
is there a place where
one may escape
from the results of evil deeds.

128
Neither in the sky
nor in mid-ocean,
nor by entering into mountain clefts,
nowhere in the world
is there a place where
one will not be overcome
by death.

Chapter 10

VIOLENCE

129

All tremble at violence;
all fear death.
Putting oneself in the place of another,
one should not kill
nor cause another to kill.

130

All tremble at violence;
life is dear to all.
Putting oneself in the place of another,
one should not kill
nor cause another to kill.

131

One who,
while himself seeking happiness,
oppresses with violence
other beings who also desire happiness,
will not attain happiness hereafter.

132

One who,
while himself seeking happiness,
does not oppress with violence
other beings who also desire happiness,
will find happiness hereafter.

133
Speak not harshly to anyone,
for those thus spoken to might retort.
Indeed, angry speech hurts,
and retaliation may overtake you.

134
If, like a broken gong,
you silence yourself,
you have approached Nibbana,
for vindictiveness is no more in you.

135
Just as a cowherd
drives the cattle to pasture with a staff,
so do old age and death
drive the life force of beings
(from existence to existence).

136
When the fool commits evil deeds,
he does not realize (their evil nature).
The witless man is tormented
by his own deeds,
like one burnt by fire.

137
He who inflicts violence
on those who are unarmed,
and offends those who are inoffensive,
will soon come upon
one of these ten states:

138-140
Sharp pain, or disaster, bodily injury,
serious illness, or derangement of mind,
trouble from the government,
or grave charges, loss of relatives,
or loss of wealth,
or houses destroyed by ravaging fire;
upon dissolution of the body
that ignorant man is born in hell.

141

Neither going about naked,
nor matted locks,
nor filth,
nor fasting,
nor lying on the ground,
nor smearing oneself
with ashes and dust,
nor sitting on the heels (in penance)
can purify a mortal
who has not overcome doubt.

142

Even though he be well-attired,
yet if he is poised, calm, controlled
and established in holy life,
having set aside violence
towards all beings—he, truly,
is a holy man,
a renunciate, a monk.

143

Only rarely is there a man
in this world who,
restrained by modesty,
avoids reproach,
as a thoroughbred horse
avoids the whip.

144

Like a thoroughbred horse
touched by the whip,
be strenuous,
be filled with spiritual yearning.
By faith and moral purity,
by effort and meditation,
by investigation of the truth,
by being rich in knowledge and virtue,
and by being mindful,
destroy this unlimited suffering.

145

Irrigators regulate the waters,
fletchers straighten arrow shafts,
carpenters shape wood,
and the good control themselves.

Chapter 11

OLD AGE

146

When this world is ever ablaze,
why this laughter, why this jubilation?
Shrouded in darkness,
will you not seek the light?

147

Behold this body—a painted image,
a mass of heaped up sores, infirm,
full of hankering—of which
nothing is lasting or stable!

148

Fully worn out is this body,
a nest of disease, and fragile.
This foul mass breaks up,
for death is the end of life.

149

These dove-coloured bones
are like gourds that lie scattered about
in autumn.
Having seen them,
how can one seek delight?

150

This city (body) is built of bones,
plastered with flesh and blood;
within are decay and death,
pride and jealousy.

151

Even gorgeous royal chariots wear out,
and indeed this body too wears out.
But the Dhamma of the Good
does not age;
thus the Good make it known
to the good.

152

The man of little learning
grows old like a bull.
He grows only in bulk, but,
his wisdom does not grow.

153

Through many a birth in samsara
have I wandered in vain,
seeking the builder of this house (of life).
Repeated birth is indeed suffering!

154

O house-builder, you are seen!
You will not build this house again.
For your rafters are broken
and your ridgepole shattered.
My mind has reached the Unconditioned;
I have attained
the destruction of craving.[19]

155
Those who in youth
have not led the holy life,
or have failed to acquire wealth,
languish like old cranes in a pond
without fish.

156
Those who in youth
have not led the holy life,
or have failed to acquire wealth,
lie sighing over the past,
like worn-out arrows (shot from) a bow.

Chapter 12

THE SELF

157

If one holds oneself dear,
one should diligently watch oneself.
Let the wise man keep vigil
during any of the three watches
of the night.[20]

158

One should first establish oneself
in what is proper;
then only should one instruct others.
Thus the wise man
will not be reproached.

159
One should do
what one teaches others to do;
if one would train others,
one should be well controlled oneself.
Difficult, indeed, is self-control.

160
One truly is the protector of oneself;
who else could the protector be?
With oneself fully controlled,
one gains a mastery
that is hard to gain.

161

The evil a witless man does by himself,
born of himself
and produced by himself,
grinds him as a diamond
grinds a hard gem.

162

Just as a jungle creeper
strangles the tree on which it grows,
even so,
a man who is exceedingly depraved
harms himself
as only an enemy might wish.

163
Easy to do are things
that are bad and harmful to oneself.
But exceedingly difficult to do are things
that are good and beneficial.

164
Whoever, on account of perverted views,
scorns the Teaching of the Perfected Ones,
the Noble and Righteous Ones—
that fool, like the bamboo,
produces fruits only for self-destruction.[21]

165

By oneself is evil done;
by oneself is one defiled.
By oneself is evil left undone;
by oneself is one made pure.
Purity and impurity depend on oneself;
no one can purify another.

166

Let one not neglect
one's own welfare
for the sake of another,
however great.
Clearly understanding
one's own welfare,
let one be intent upon the good.

Chapter 13

THE WORLD

167

Follow not the vulgar way;
live not in heedlessness;
hold not false views;
linger not long in worldly existence.

168

Arise! Do not be heedless!
Lead a righteous life.
The righteous live happily
both in this world and the next.

169

Lead a righteous life;
lead not a base life.
The righteous live happily
both in this world and the next.

170

One who looks upon the world
as a bubble and a mirage,
him the King of Death sees not.

171
Come! Behold this world,
which is like a decorated royal chariot.
Here fools flounder,
but the wise have no attachment to it.

172
He who having been heedless
is heedless no more,
illuminates this world
like the moon freed from clouds.

173
He who by good deeds
covers the evil he has done,
illuminates this world
like the moon freed from clouds.

174
Blind is this world;
here only a few possess insight.
Only a few, like birds escaping from a net,
go to the realms of bliss.

175

Swans fly on the path of the sun;
men pass through the air
by psychic powers;
the wise are led away from the world
after vanquishing Mara and his host.

176

For a liar who has violated
the one law (of truthfulness),
who holds in scorn the hereafter,
there is no evil that he cannot do.

177
Truly, misers fare
not to heavenly realms;
nor, indeed, do fools praise generosity.
But the wise man rejoices in giving,
and by that alone does he become
happy hereafter.

178
Better than sole sovereignty
over the earth,
better than going to heaven,
better even than lordship
over all the worlds
is the supramundane
Fruition of Stream Entrance.[22]

Chapter 14

THE BUDDHA

179
By what track can you trace
that trackless Buddha of limitless range,
whose victory nothing can undo,
whom none of the vanquished defilements
can ever pursue?

180
By what track can you trace
that trackless Buddha of limitless range,
in whom exists no longer
the entangling and embroiling craving
that perpetuates becoming?

181
Those wise ones who are devoted
to meditation and who delight
in the calm of renunciation—
such mindful ones,
Supreme Buddhas,
even the gods hold dear.

182
Hard is it to be born a man;
hard is the life of mortals.
Hard is it to gain the opportunity
of hearing the Sublime Truth,
and hard to encounter
is the arising of the Buddhas.

183

To avoid all evil,
to cultivate good,
and to cleanse one's mind—
this is the teaching of the Buddhas.

184

Enduring patience
is the highest austerity.
"Nibbana is supreme," say the Buddhas.
He is not a true monk
who harms another,
nor a true renunciate
who oppresses others.

185
Not despising,
not harming,
restraint according
to the code of monastic discipline,
moderation in food,
dwelling in solitude,
devotion to meditation—
this is the teaching of the Buddhas.

186-187

There is no satisfying sensual desires,
    even with a rain of gold coins.
        For sensual pleasures
give little satisfaction and much pain.
        Having understood this,
        the wise man finds no delight
            even in heavenly pleasures.
The disciple of the Supreme Buddha
delights in the destruction of craving.

188
Driven only by fear,
do men go for refuge to many places—
to hills, woods, groves,
trees and shrines.

189
Such, indeed, is no safe refuge;
such is not the refuge supreme.
Not by resorting to such a refuge
is one released from all suffering.

190-191

He who has gone for refuge
to the Buddha,
his Teaching and his Order,
penetrates with transcendental wisdom
the Four Noble Truths—
suffering,
the cause of suffering,
the cessation of suffering,
and the Noble Eightfold Path
leading to the cessation of suffering.[23]

192

This indeed is the safe refuge,
this is the refuge supreme.
Having gone to such a refuge,
one is released from all suffering.

193

Hard to find is the thoroughbred man
(the Buddha); he is not born everywhere.
Where such a wise man is born,
that clan thrives happily.

194
Blessed is the birth of the Buddhas;
blessed is the enunciation
of the sacred Teaching;
blessed is the harmony in the Order,
and blessed is the spiritual pursuit
of the united truth-seekers.

195-196

He who reveres
those worthy of reverence,
the Buddhas and their disciples,
who have transcended all obstacles
and passed beyond the reach of sorrow
and lamentation—
he who reveres
such peaceful and fearless ones,
his merit none can compute
by any measure.

Chapter 15

HAPPINESS

197

Happy indeed we live,
friendly amidst the hostile.
Amidst hostile men
we dwell free from hatred.

198

Happy indeed we live,
unafflicted amidst the afflicted
(by craving).
Amidst afflicted men
we dwell free from affliction.

199

Happy indeed we live,
free from avarice
amidst the avaricious.
Amidst avaricious men
we dwell free from avarice.

200

Happy indeed we live,
we who possess nothing.
Feeders on joy we shall be,
like the Radiant Gods.

201

Victory begets enmity;
the defeated dwell in pain.
Happily the peaceful live,
discarding both victory and defeat.

202

There is no fire like lust
and no crime like hatred.
There is no ill
like the aggregates (of existence)
and no bliss higher
than the peace (of Nibbana).[24]

203
Hunger is the worst disease,
conditioned things the worst suffering.
Knowing this as it really is,
the wise realize Nibbana,
the highest bliss.[25]

204
Health is the precious gain
and contentment the greatest wealth.
A trustworthy person is the best kinsman,
Nibbana the highest bliss.

205
Having savoured
the taste of solitude and peace
(of Nibbana),
pain-free and stainless he becomes,
drinking deep
the taste of the bliss of Truth.

206
Good it is to see the Noble Ones;
to live with them is ever blissful.
One will always be happy
by not encountering fools.

207
Indeed,
he who moves
in the company of fools
grieves for long.
Association with fools is ever painful,
like partnership with an enemy.
But association
with the wise is happy,
like meeting one's own kinsmen.

208
Therefore,
follow the Noble One,
who is steadfast, wise, learned,
dutiful and devout.
One should follow
only such a man,
who is truly good and discerning,
even as the moon
follows the path of the stars.

Chapter 16

AFFECTION

209

Giving himself to things
to be shunned
and not exerting
where exertion is needed,
a seeker after pleasures,
having given up his true welfare,
envies those intent upon theirs.

210

Seek no intimacy
with the beloved
and also not with the unloved,
for not to see the beloved
and to see the unloved,
both are painful.

211
Therefore,
hold nothing dear,
for separation from the dear is painful.
There are no bonds for those who have nothing
beloved or unloved.

212
From endearment springs grief,
from endearment springs fear.
For him who is wholly free
from endearment
there is no grief,
whence then fear?

213

From affection springs grief,
from affection springs fear.
For him who is wholly free
from affection
there is no grief,
whence then fear?

214

From attachment springs grief,
from attachment springs fear.
For him who is wholly free
from attachment there is no grief,
whence then fear?

215

From lust springs grief,
from lust springs fear.
For him who is wholly free
from lust
there is no grief,
whence then fear?

216

From craving springs grief,
from craving springs fear.
For him who is wholly free
from craving
there is no grief;
whence then fear?

217

People hold dear him
who embodies virtue and insight,
who is principled,
has realized the truth,
and who himself
does what he ought to be doing.

218

One who is intent upon the
Ineffable (Nibbana),
dwells with mind inspired
(by supramundane wisdom),
and is no more bound by sense pleasures –
such a man is called
"One Bound Upstream".[26]

219
When, after a long absence,
a man safely returns home
from afar,
his relatives, friends
and well-wishers
welcome him home on arrival.

220
As kinsmen
welcome a dear one on arrival,
even so his own good deeds
will welcome the doer of good
who has gone from this world
to the next.

Chapter 17

ANGER

221

One should give up anger,
renounce pride,
and overcome all fetters.
Suffering never befalls him
who clings not to mind and body
and is detached.

222

He who checks
rising anger as a charioteer
checks a rolling chariot,
him I call a true charioteer.
Others only hold the reins.

223

Overcome the angry by non-anger;
overcome the wicked by goodness;
overcome the miser by generosity;
overcome the liar by truth.

224

Speak the truth; yield not to anger;
when asked,
give even if you only have a little.
By these three means
can one reach the presence of the gods.

225
Those sages who are inoffensive
and ever restrained in body,
go to the Deathless State,
where, having gone,
they grieve no more.

226
Those who are ever vigilant,
who discipline themselves
day and night,
and are ever intent upon Nibbana—
their defilements fade away.

227
O Atula!
Indeed, this is an ancient practice,
not one only of today:
they blame those who remain silent,
they blame those who speak much,
they blame those who speak in moderation.
There is none in this world
who is not blamed.

228
There never was,
there never will be,
nor is there now,
a person who is wholly blamed
or wholly praised.

229
But the man whom the wise praise,
after observing him day after day,
is one of flawless character,
wise, and endowed
with knowledge and virtue.

230
Who can blame such a one,
as worthy as a coin of refined gold?
Even the gods praise him;
by Brahma, too, is he praised.

231

Let a man guard himself
against irritability in bodily action;
let him be controlled in deed.
Abandoning bodily misconduct,
let him practise good conduct in deed.

232

Let a man guard himself
against irritability in speech;
let him be controlled in speech.
Abandoning verbal misconduct,
let him practise good conduct in speech.

233

Let a man guard himself
against irritability in thought;
let him be controlled in mind.
Abandoning mental misconduct,
let him practise good conduct
in thought.

234

The wise are controlled
in bodily action,
controlled in speech
and controlled in thought.
They are truly well-controlled.

Chapter 18

IMPURITY

235

Like a withered leaf are you now;
death's messengers await you.
You stand on the eve of your departure,
yet you have made no provision
for your journey!

236

Make an island for yourself!
Strive hard and become wise!
Rid of impurities and cleansed of stain,
you shall enter the celestial abode
of the Noble Ones.

237
Your life has come to an end now;
you are setting forth into the presence
of Yama, the king of death.
No resting place is there for you
on the way,
yet you have made no provision
for your journey!

238
Make an island for yourself!
Strive hard and become wise!
Rid of impurities and cleansed of stain,
you shall not come again
to birth and decay.

239
One by one,
little by little,
moment by moment,
a wise man should remove
his own impurities,
as a smith removes the dross from silver.

240
Just as rust arising from iron
eats away the base from which it arises,
even so,
their own deeds lead transgressors
to states of woe.

241

Non-repetition
is the bane of scriptures;
neglect is the bane of a home;
slovenliness is the bane
of personal appearance,
and heedlessness is the bane
of a guard.

242
Unchastity is the taint in a woman;
niggardliness is the taint in a giver.
Taints, indeed,
are all evil things,
both in this world and the next.

243
A worse taint than these
is ignorance,
the worst of all taints.
Destroy this one taint
and become taintless, O monks!

244
Easy is life for the shameless
one who is as impudent as a crow,
is backbiting and forward,
arrogant and corrupt.

245
Difficult is life for the modest one
who always seeks purity,
is detached and unassuming,
clean in life,
and discerning.

246-247
One who destroys life,
utters lies, takes what is not given,
goes to another man's wife,
and is addicted to intoxicating drinks—
such a man digs up his own root
even in this very world.

248
Know this, O good man:
evil things are difficult to control.
Let not greed and wickedness
drag you to protracted misery.

249
People give
according to their faith or regard.
If one becomes discontented
with the food and drink given by others,
one does not attain meditative absorption,
either by day or by night.

250
But he in whom
this(discontent) is fully destroyed,
uprooted and extinct,
he attains absorption,
both by day and by night.

251

There is no fire like lust;
there is no grip like hatred;
there is no net like delusion;
there is no river like craving.

252

Easily seen is the fault of others,
but one's own is difficult to see.
Like chaff one winnows another's faults,
but hides one's own,
even as a crafty fowler
hides behind sham branches.

253
He who seeks another's faults,
who is ever censorious—
his cankers grow.
He is far from destruction of the cankers.

254
There is no track in the sky,
and no recluse outside
(the Buddha's dispensation).
Mankind delights in worldliness,
but the Buddhas
are free from worldliness.[27]

255
There is no track in the sky,
and no recluse outside
(the Buddha's dispensation).
There are no conditioned things
that are eternal,
and no instability in the Buddhas.

Chapter 19

THE JUST

256

Not by passing arbitrary judgements
does a man become just;
a wise man is he
who investigates
both right and wrong.

257

He who does not judge
others arbitrarily,
but passes judgement impartially
according to truth,
that sagacious man is a guardian of law
and is called just.

258
One is not wise
because one speaks much.
He who is peaceable,
friendly and fearless is called wise.

259
A man is not versed in Dhamma
because he speaks much.
He who,
after hearing even a little Dhamma,
realizes its truth directly
and is not heedless of it,
is truly versed in the Dhamma.

260

A monk is not an Elder
because his head is gray.
He is but ripe in age,
and he is called one grown old in vain.

261

One in whom there is truthfulness,
virtue, inoffensiveness,
restraint and self-mastery,
who is free from defilements
and is wise—he is truly called an Elder.

262
Not by mere eloquence
nor by beauty of form
does a man become accomplished,
if he is jealous, selfish and deceitful.

263
But he in whom
these are wholly destroyed,
uprooted and extinct,
and who has cast out hatred—
that wise man is truly accomplished.

264

Not by shaven head
does a man
who is indisciplined and untruthful
become a monk.
How can he who is full of desire and greed
be a monk?

265

He who wholly subdues
evil both small and great
is called a monk,
because he has overcome all evil.

266
He is not a monk
just because he lives on others' alms.
Not by adopting outward form
does one become a true monk.

267
Whoever here (in the Dispensation)
lives the holy life,
transcending both merit and demerit,
and walks with understanding
in this world—he is truly called a monk.

268

Not by observing silence
does one become a sage,
if he be foolish and ignorant.
But that man is wise who,
as if holding a balance-scale,
accepts only the good.

269
The sage, (thus) rejecting the evil,
is truly a sage.
Since he comprehends both
(present and future) worlds,
he is called a sage.

270
He is not noble
who injures living beings.
He is called noble because
he is harmless towards all living beings.

271-272

Not by rules and observances,
not even by much learning,
nor by gain of absorption,
nor by a life of seclusion,
nor by thinking,
"I enjoy the bliss of renunciation,
which is not experienced
by the worldling"
should you, O monks,
rest content,
until the utter destruction of cankers
(Arahatship) is reached.

Chapter 20

THE PATH

273
Of all paths
the Eightfold Path is the best;
of all truths
the Four Noble Truths are the best;
of all things
passionlessness is the best;
of men the Seeing One (the Buddha)
is the best.[28]

274
This is the only path;
there is none other for the purification
of insight.
Tread this path,
and you will bewilder Mara.

275

Walking upon this path
you will make an end of suffering.
Having discovered
how to pull out the thorn of lust,
I make known the path.

276

You yourselves must strive;
the Buddhas[29] only point the way.
Those meditative ones who tread the path
are released from the bonds of Mara.

277
"All conditioned things are impermanent"
—when one sees this with wisdom,
one turns away from suffering.
This is the path to purification.

278
"All conditioned things are unsatisfactory"
—when one sees this with wisdom,
one turns away from suffering.
This is the path to purification.

279
"All things are not-self"—
when one sees this with wisdom,
one turns away from suffering.
This is the path to purification.

280
The idler who does not exert himself
when he should,
who though young and strong
is full of sloth,
with a mind full of vain thoughts—
such an indolent man
does not find the path to wisdom.

281

Let a man be watchful of speech,
 well controlled in mind,
and not commit evil in bodily action.
Let him purify
 these three courses of action,
 and win the path
made known by the Great Sage.[30]

282

Wisdom springs from meditation;
without meditation wisdom wanes.
Having known these
two paths of progress and decline,
let a man so conduct himself
that his wisdom may increase.

283

Cut down the forest (lust),
but not the tree;
from the forest springs fear.
Having cut down the forest
and the under-brush (desire),
be passionless, O monks![31]

284

For so long as the underbrush of desire,
even the most subtle,
of a man towards a woman
is not cut down,
his mind is in bondage,
like the sucking calf to its mother.

285

Cut off your affection in the manner
a man plucks with his hand
an autumn lotus.
Cultivate only the path to peace,
Nibbana, as made known
by the Exalted One.

286

"Here shall I live during the rains,
here in winter and summer"—
thus thinks the fool.
He does not realize the danger
(that death might intervene).

287

As a great flood carries away
a sleeping village,
so death seizes and carries away
the man with a clinging mind,
doting on his children and cattle.

288

For him who is assailed by death
there is no protection by kinsmen.
None there are to save him—
no sons, nor father nor relatives.

289
Realizing this fact,
let the wise man,
restrained by morality,
hasten to clear the path
leading to Nibbana.

Chapter 21

MISCELLANEOUS

290

If by renouncing
a lesser happiness
one may realize a greater happiness,
let the wise man renounce the lesser,
having regard for the greater.

291

Entangled by the bonds of hate,
he who seeks his own happiness
by inflicting pain on others,
is never delivered from hatred.

292

The cankers only increase
for those who are
arrogant and heedless,
who leave undone what should be done
and do what should not be done.

293

The cankers cease for those
mindful and clearly comprehending ones
who always earnestly practise mindfulness
of the body, who do not resort
to what should not be done,
and steadfastly pursue what should be done.

294

Having slain mother (craving),
father (self-conceit),
two warrior kings
(eternalism and nihilism),
and destroyed a country
(sense organs and sense objects)
together with its treasurer
(attachment and lust),
ungrieving goes the holy man.

295

Having slain mother, father,
two brahmin kings (two extreme views),
and a tiger as the fifth
(the five mental hindrances),
ungrieving goes the holy man.

296

Those disciples of Gotama
ever awaken happily
who day and night
constantly practise the
Recollection of the Qualities of the Buddha.

297

Those disciples of Gotama
ever awaken happily who day and night
constantly practise the
Recollection of the
Qualities of the Dhamma.

298
Those disciples of Gotama
ever awaken happily
who day and night
constantly practise
the Recollection of the Qualities
of the Sangha.

299
Those disciples of Gotama
ever awaken happily
who day and night
constantly practise
Mindfulness of the Body.

300

Those disciples of Gotama
ever awaken happily
whose minds by day and night
delight in the practice of non-violence.

301

Those disciples of Gotama
ever awaken happily
whose minds by day and night
delight in the practice of meditation.

302

Difficult is life as a monk;
difficult is it to delight therein.
Also difficult and sorrowful
is household life.
Suffering comes from association
with unequals;
suffering comes from wandering
in samsara.
Therefore,
be not an aimless wanderer,
be not a pursuer of suffering.

303
He who is full of faith and virtue,
and possessess good repute and wealth—
he is respected everywhere,
in whatever land he travels.

304
The good shine even from afar,
like the Himalayan mountain.
But the wicked are unseen,
like arrows shot in the night.

305

He who sits alone,
sleeps alone and walks alone,
who is strenuous and subdues
himself alone,
will find delight
in the solitude of the forest.

Chapter 22

THE STATE OF WOE

306
The liar goes to the state of woe;
also he who, having done (wrong),
says, "I did not do it."
Men of base actions both,
on departing they share the same destiny
in the other world.

307
There are many evil characters
and uncontrolled men
wearing the saffron robe.
These wicked men will be born
in states of woe
because of their evil deeds.

308

It would be better to swallow
a red-hot iron ball,
blazing like fire,
than
as an immoral and uncontrolled monk
to eat the alms of the people.

309

Four misfortunes befall the reckless man
who consorts with another's wife:
acquisition of demerit,
disturbed sleep,
ill-repute
and (rebirth in) states of woe.

310
Such a man acquires
demerit and an unhappy birth
in the future.
Brief is the pleasure
of the frightened man and woman,
and the king imposes heavy punishment.
Hence,
let no man consort with another's wife.

311
Just as kusa grass wrongly handled
cuts the hand,
even so, a recluse's life wrongly lived
drags one to states of woe.

312
Any loose act,
any corrupt observance,
any life of questionable celibacy—
none of these bear much fruit.

313
If anything is to be done,
let one do it with sustained vigor.
A lax monastic life
stirs up the dust of passions all the more.

314

An evil deed is better left undone,
for such a deed torments one afterwards.
But a good deed is better done,
doing which one repents not later.

315

Just as a border city is closely guarded
both within and without,
even so, guard yourself.
Do not let slip this opportunity
(for spiritual growth).
For those who let slip this opportunity
grieve indeed when consigned to hell.[32]

316

Those who are ashamed
of what they should not be ashamed of,
and are not ashamed
of what they should be ashamed of—
upholding false views,
they go to states of woe.

317

Those who see something
to fear where there is nothing to fear,
and see nothing
to fear where there is something to fear—
upholding false views,
they go to states of woe.

318

Those who imagine evil
where there is none,
and do not see evil where it is—
upholding false views,
they go to states of woe.

319

Those who discern
the wrong as wrong
and the right as right—
upholding right views,
they go to realms of bliss.

Chapter 23

THE ELEPHANT

320
As an elephant in the battlefield
withstands arrows
shot from bows all around,
even so shall I endure abuse.
There are many, indeed, who lack virtue.

321
A tamed elephant is led into a crowd,
and the king mounts a tamed elephant.
Best among men is the subdued
one who endures abuse.

322
Excellent are well-trained mules,
thoroughbred Sindhu horses
and noble tusker elephants.
But better still is the man
who has subdued himself.

323
Not by these mounts, however,
would one go to the
Untrodden Land (Nibbana),
as one who is self-tamed
goes by his own tamed
and well-controlled mind.

324
Musty during rut,
the tusker named Dhanapalaka
is uncontrollable.
Held in captivity,
the tusker does not touch a morsel,
but only longingly calls to mind
the elephant forest.

325
When a man
is sluggish and gluttonous,
sleeping and rolling around in bed
like a fat domestic pig,
that sluggard undergoes
rebirth again and again.

326

Formerly this mind wandered
about as it liked,
where it wished
and according to its pleasure,
but now I shall thoroughly master it
with wisdom
as a mahout controls with his ankus
an elephant in rut.

327

Delight in heedfulness!
Guard well your thoughts!
Draw yourself out of this bog of evil,
even as an elephant
draws himself out of the mud.

328
If for company
you find a wise and prudent friend
who leads a good life,
you should, overcoming all impediments,
keep his company joyously and mindfully.

329
If for company
you cannot find a wise and prudent friend
who leads a good life,
then, like a king who leaves behind
a conquered kingdom,
or like a lone elephant
in the elephant forest,
you should go your way alone.

330
Better it is to live alone;
there is no fellowship with a fool.
Live alone and do no evil;
be carefree like an elephant
in the elephant forest.

331
Good are friends when need arises;
good is contentment
with just what one has;
good is merit when life is at an end,
and good is the abandoning
of all suffering (through Arahatship).

332

In this world,
good it is to serve one's mother,
good it is to serve one's father,
good it is to serve the monks,
and good it is to serve the holy men.

333

Good is virtue until life's end,
good is faith that is steadfast,
good is the acquisition of wisdom,
and good is the avoidance of evil.

Chapter 24

CRAVING

334
The craving of one given to heedless living
grows like a creeper.
Like the monkey seeking fruits
in the forest,
he leaps from life to life
(tasting the fruit of his kamma).

335
Whoever is overcome
by this wretched and sticky craving,
his sorrows grow
like grass after the rains.

336
But whoever overcomes
this wretched craving,
so difficult to overcome,
from him sorrows fall away
like water from a lotus leaf.

337
This I say to you:
Good luck to all assembled here!
Dig up the root of craving,
like one in search of the fragrant roots
of birana grass.
Let not Mara crush you
again and again,
as a flood crushes a reed.

338

Just as a tree,
though cut down,
sprouts up again if its roots
remain uncut and firm,
even so, until the craving
that lies dormant is rooted out,
suffering springs up again and again.

339

The misguided man
in whom the thirty-six currents
of craving strongly rush toward
pleasurable objects,
is swept away by the flood
of his passionate thoughts.[33]

340

Everywhere these currents flow,
and the creeper (of craving)
sprouts and grows.
Seeing that the creeper has sprung up,
cut off its root with wisdom.

341

Flowing in (from all objects)
and watered by craving,
feelings of pleasure arise in beings.
Bent on pleasures and seeking enjoyment,
these men fall prey to birth and decay.

342
Beset by craving,
people run about
like an entrapped hare.
Held fast by mental fetters,
they come to suffering again and again
for a long time.

343
Beset by craving,
people run about
like an entrapped hare.
Therefore,
one who yearns to be passion-free
should destroy his own craving.

344
There is one who,
turning away from desire
(for household life)
takes to the life of the forest
(i.e., of a monk).
But after being freed from the household,
he runs back to it.
Behold that man!
Though freed,
he runs back to that very bondage!

345-346

That is not a strong fetter,
the wise say,
which is made of iron,
wood or hemp.
But the infatuation and longing
for jewels and ornaments,
children and wives—that,
they say, is a far stronger fetter,
which pulls one downward and,
though seemingly loose,
is hard to remove.
This, too, the wise cut off.
Giving up sensual pleasure,
and without any longing,
they renounce the world.

347
Those who are lust-infatuated
fall back into the swirling current
(of samsara)
like a spider on its self-spun web.
This, too, the wise cut off.
Without any longing,
they abandon all suffering
and renounce the world.

348

Let go of the past,
let go of the future,
let go of the present,
and cross over
to the farther shore of existence.
With mind wholly liberated,
you shall come no more to birth and death.

349

For a person tormented
by evil thoughts,
who is passion-dominated
and given to the pursuit of pleasure,
his craving steadily grows.
He makes the fetter strong indeed.

350

He who delights
in subduing evil thoughts,
who meditates on the impurities
and is ever mindful—
it is he who will make an end of craving
and rend asunder Mara's fetter.

351

He who has reached the goal,
is fearless, free from craving,
passionless,
and has plucked out the thorns
of existence—for him this is the last body.

352
He who is free
from craving and attachment,
is perfect in uncovering
the true meaning of the Teaching,
and knows the arrangement
of the sacred texts in correct sequence—
he, indeed,
is the bearer of his final body.
He is truly called the profoundly wise one,
the great man.

353
A victor am I over all,
all have I known.
Yet unattached am I
to all that is conquered and known.
Abandoning all,
I am freed
through the destruction of craving.
Having thus directly comprehended
all by myself,
whom shall I call my teacher?

354

The gift of Dhamma excels all gifts;
the taste of Dhamma excels all tastes;
the delight in Dhamma excels all delights.
The Craving-Freed vanquishes all suffering.

355

Riches ruin only the foolish,
not those in quest of the Beyond.
By craving for riches
the witless man ruins himself
as well as others.

356
Weeds are the bane of fields,
lust is the bane of mankind.
Therefore,
what is offered to those
free of lust
yields abundant fruit.

357
Weeds are the bane of fields,
hatred is the bane of mankind.
Therefore, what is offered to those
free of hatred
yields abundant fruit.

358

Weeds are the bane of fields,
delusion is the bane of mankind.
Therefore, what is offered to those
free of delusion
yields abundant fruit.

359

Weeds are the bane of fields,
desire is the bane of mankind.
Therefore, what is offered to those
free of desire
yields abundant fruit.

Chapter 25

THE MONK

360

Good is restraint over the eye;
good is restraint over the ear;
good is restraint over the nose;
good is restraint over the tongue.

361

Good is restraint in the body;
good is restraint in speech;
good is restraint in thought.
Restraint everywhere is good.
The monk restrained in every way
is freed from all suffering.

362
He who has control
over his hands, feet and tongue;
who is fully controlled,
delights in inward development,
is absorbed in meditation,
keeps to himself and is contented—
him do people call a monk.

363
That monk who has control
over his tongue, is moderate in speech,
unassuming and who explains the Teaching
in both letter and spirit—
whatever he says is pleasing.

364

The monk who abides in the Dhamma,
delights in the Dhamma,
meditates on the Dhamma
and bears the Dhamma well in mind,
he does not fall away
from the sublime Dhamma.

365

One should not despise
what one has received,
nor envy the gains of others.
The monk who envies the gains of others
does not attain to meditative absorption.

366

A monk who does not despise
what he has received,
even though it be little,
who is pure in livelihood
and unremitting in effort,
him even the gods praise.

367

He who has no attachment
whatsoever for the mind and body,
who does not grieve for what he has not
—he is truly called a monk.

368

The monk who abides
in universal love and is deeply devoted
to the Teaching of the Buddha
attains the peace of Nibbana,
the bliss of the cessation
of all conditioned things.

369

Empty this boat,
O monk! Emptied, it will sail lightly.
Rid of lust and hatred,
you shall reach Nibbana.

370

Cut off the five,
abandon the five,
and cultivate the five.
The monk who has overcome
the five bonds
is called one who has crossed the flood.[34]

371

Meditate, O monk!
Do not be heedless.
Let not your mind
whirl on sensual pleasures.
Heedless, do not swallow a red hot iron ball,
lest you cry when burning,
"O this is painful!"

372

There is no meditative concentration
for him who lacks insight,
and no insight for him
who lacks meditative concentration.
He in whom are found both
meditative concentration and insight,
indeed, is close to Nibbana.

373

The monk who has retired
to a solitary abode and calmed his mind,
who comprehends the Dhamma
with insight,
in him there arises a delight
that transcends all human delights.

374

Whenever he sees with insight
the rise and fall of the aggregates,
he is full of joy and happiness.
To the discerning one
this reflects the Deathless.[35]

375

Control of the senses,
contentment,
restraint according to the code of
monastic discipline—
these form the basis of holy life
here for the wise monk.

376
Let him associate with friends
who are noble,
energetic and pure in life,
let him be cordial
and refined in conduct.
Thus, full of joy,
he will make an end of suffering.

377

Just as the jasmine creeper
sheds its withered flowers,
even so,
O monks,
should you totally shed
lust and hatred!

378

The monk who is calm in body,
calm in speech, calm in thought,
well composed
and who has spewn out worldliness—
he, truly, is called serene.

379

By oneself
one must censure oneself
and scrutinize oneself.
The self-guarded and mindful monk
will always live in happiness.

380

One is one's own protector,
one is one's own refuge.
Therefore,
one should control oneself,
even as the trader controls a noble steed.

381

Full of joy, full of faith
in the Teaching of the Buddha,
the monk attains the Peaceful State,
the bliss of cessation
of conditioned things.

382

That monk who while young
devotes himself to the
Teaching of the Buddha
illumines this world
like the moon freed from clouds.

Chapter 26

THE HOLY MAN

383

Exert yourself, O holy man!
Cut off the stream (of craving),
and discard sense desires.
Knowing the destruction
of all conditioned things, become,
O holy man,
the knower of the Uncreate (Nibbana)![36]

384

When a holy man
has reached
the summit of the two paths
(meditative concentration and insight),
he knows the truth
and all his fetters fall away.

385

He for whom
there is neither this shore
nor the other shore,
nor yet both,
he who is free of cares and is unfettered
—him do I call a holy man.[37]

386

He who is meditative,
stainless and settled,
whose work is done
and who is free from cankers,
having reached the highest goal—
him do I call a holy man.

387

The sun shines by day,
the moon shines by night.
The warrior shines in armour,
the holy man shines in meditation.
But the Buddha shines
resplendent all day and all night.

388

Because he has discarded evil,
he is called a holy man.
Because he is serene in conduct,
he is called a recluse.
And because he has renounced
his impurities,
he is called a renunciate.

389
One should not strike a holy man,
nor should a holy man,
when struck, give way to anger.
Shame on him who strikes a holy man,
and more shame on him
who gives way to anger.

390
Nothing is better for a holy man
than when he holds his mind back
from what is endearing.
To the extent the intent to harm wears away,
to that extent does suffering subside.

391
He who does no evil
in deed, word and thought,
who is restrained in these three ways—
him do I call a holy man.

392
Just as a brahmin priest
reveres his sacrificial fire,
even so should one devoutly revere
the person from whom one has learned
the Dhamma
taught by the Buddha.

393

Not by matted hair, nor by lineage,
nor by birth does one become a holy man.
But he in whom
truth and righteousness exist—
he is pure, he is a holy man.

394

What is the use of your matted hair,
O witless man?
What of your garment of antelope's hide?
Within you is the tangle (of passion);
Only outwardly do you cleanse yourself.[38]

395

The person who wears
a robe made of rags, who is lean,
with veins showing all over the body,
and who meditates alone in the forest—
him do I call a holy man.

396

I do not call him a holy man
because of his lineage or high-born mother.
If he is full of impeding attachments,
he is just a supercilious man.
But who is free from impediments
and clinging—
him do I call a holy man.

397
He who, having cut off all fetters,
trembles no more,
who has overcome all attachments
and is emancipated—
him do I call a holy man.

398

He who has cut off the thong (of hatred),
the band (of craving),
and the rope (of false views),
together with the appurtenances
(latent evil tendencies),
he who has removed the crossbar
(of ignorance)
and is enlightened—
him do I call a holy man.

399
He who without resentment
endures abuse,
beating and punishment;
whose power,
real might, is patience—
him do I call a holy man.

400
He who is free from anger,
is devout, virtuous, without craving,
selfsubdued and bears his final body—
him I call a holy man.

401

Like water on a lotus leaf,
or a mustard seed
on the point of a needle,
he who does not cling to sensual pleasures—
him do I call a holy man.

402

He who in this very life
realizes for himself the end of suffering,
who has laid aside the burden
and become emancipated—
him do I call a holy man.

403

He who has profound knowledge,
who is wise,
skilled in discerning
the right or wrong path,
and has reached the highest goal—
him do I call a holy man.

404

He who holds aloof
from house holders and ascetics alike,
and wanders about
with no fixed abode
and but few wants—
him do I call a holy man.

405

He who has renounced violence
towards all living beings,
weak or strong,
who neither kills nor causes others to kill—
him do I call a holy man.

406

He who is friendly amidst the hostile,
peaceful amidst the violent,
and unattached amidst the attached—
him do I call a holy man.

407

He whose lust and hatred,
pride and hypocrisy
have fallen off like a mustard seed
from the point of a needle—
him do I call a holy man.

408

He who utters gentle,
instructive and truthful words,
who imprecates none—
him do I call a holy man.

409

He who in this world
takes nothing that is not given to him,
be it long or short,
small or big,
good or bad—
him do I call a holy man.

410

He who wants nothing
of either this world or the next,
who is desire-free and emancipated—
him do I call a holy man.

411
He who has no attachment,
who through perfect knowledge
is free from doubts
and has plunged into the Deathless—
him do I call a holy man.

412
He who in this world
has transcended the ties
of both merit and demerit,
who is sorrowless, stainless and pure—
him do I call a holy man.

413

He who,
like the moon,
is spotless and pure, serene and clear,
who has destroyed the delight in existence—
him do I call a holy man.

414

He who,
having traversed this miry,
perilous and delusive round of existence,
has crossed over
and reached the other shore;
who is meditative, calm, free from doubt,
and, clinging to nothing,
has attained to Nibbana—
him do I call a holy man.

415
He who,
having abandoned sensual pleasures,
has renounced the household life
and become a homeless one;
has destroyed both sensual desire
and continued existence—
him do I call a holy man.

416
He who,
having abandoned craving,
has renounced the household life
and become a homeless one,
has destroyed both craving
and continued existence—
him do I call a holy man.

417
He who,
casting off human bonds
and transcending heavenly ties,
is wholly delivered of all bondages—
him do I call a holy man.

418
He who,
having cast off likes and dislikes,
has become tranquil,
is rid of the substrata of existence
and like a hero
has conquered all the worlds—
him do I call a holy man.

419
He who in every way
knows the death and rebirth of all beings,
and is totally detached,
blessed and enlightened—
him do I call a holy man.

420
He whose track no gods,
no angels, no humans trace,
the Arahat who has destroyed
all cankers—him do I call a holy man.

421

He who clings to nothing
of the past, present and future,
who has no attachment
and holds on to nothing—
him do I call a holy man.

422

He, the Noble, the Excellent,
the Heroic, the Great Sage,
the Conqueror, the Passionless,
the Pure, the Enlightened one—
him do I call a holy man.

423
He who knows his former births,
who sees heaven and hell,
who has reached the end of births
and attained to the perfection of insight,
the sage who has reached
the summit of spiritual excellence—
him do I call a holy man.

Notes

1. *Law Eternal (Dhammo Sanantano):*
   Law is natural principle, timeless norm, what works on its original power requiring no extraneous support. By its own nature hatred only generates and never appeases hatred.

2. *Mara:*
   Literally, the destroyer; Mara stands for 1) mental defilements; 2) phenomenal world; 3) death (no. 1 leads to 2 and 3); 4) Lord of evil forces—a powerful deity who tempts and misleads those following the path to Nibbana.

3. Meditating on the impurities *(Asubhanupassim)*; techniques of meditation which reveal the inherent impurity or repulsiveness of the body, and act as powerful antidotes to lust.

4. *Realms of woe (duggati):*
   The worlds of demons, ghosts, animals and the hells.

5. *Realms of bliss (sugati):*
   These consist of 1) human and six divine planes of the realms of desire; 2) sixteen planes of the radiant brahma deities of subtle form; 3) four planes of formless (pure mental) brahma deities.

6. *The Deathless (amata):*
   Nibbana is deathless because those who attain it are free from the cycle of repeated birth and death.

7. *The Noble Ones (ariya):*
   Those who have reached any of the four stages of supramundane

attainment leading irreversibly to Nibbana. The resort *(gocara)* of the Noble Ones are the 37 Requisites of Enlightenment (Bodhi-pakkhiya dhamma).

8   *Cave:*
    Heart is the seat of consciousness. Hence the analogy of the mind resting in the cave of the heart. Every moment of consciousness arises, continues and passes by itself, not together with other moments; hence "alone".

9   *Beyond both merit and demerit:*
    The Arahat having abandoned all defilements, can no longer perform evil actions; having no more attachment to any plane of existence his virtuous actions no longer bear karmic fruit.

10 *Yama:*
    Another name for Mara as king of death and ruler of the states of woe.

11 *Striver-on-the-Path (Sekha):*
    One who has achieved any of the first three stages of supramundane attainment: a Stream-enterer, Once-returner and Non-returner. Sekho perfects the path of wisdom (37 Bodhipakkhiya dhamma).

12 Sage collects alms in the village and provides others the opportunity to gain merit *(puñña)*.

13 Fragrance of virtue pervades everywhere.
    Tagara: is a fragrant flowering shrub.

14 *Ripened:*
    Karmic result is not always immediate, but may fructify in a future lifetime.

15 *Cankers (asava)*:

The four basic mental pollutants of sensual desire, desire for continued existence, ignorance and false views. Their destruction is necessary for attainment of Nibbana.

16 *Ties (gantha)*:

Four bonds of covetousness, ill-will, blind adherence to rules and rituals and dogmatic bigotry.

17 *Accumulates* includes accumulation of kamma.

Food: refers to physical nutriment, sensory impressions, volitional activity and rebirth consciousness, all of which feed the process of continued existence.

18 *Brahma*: A high divinity in Indian religions.

19 According to the commentary, these verses are the Buddha's "Song of Victory", his first utterance after Enlightenment. *House-builder*: craving; *house*: samsaric existence; *rafters*: passions; *ridgepole*: ignorance.

20 *Three watches*: Youth, middle age and old age.

21 Bamboos perish immediately after producing fruits.

22 *Stream-entry (Sotapatti)*:

First stage of supramundane attainment.

23 *The Order*:

The Order of Noble Ones who have reached the four supramundane stages, and the monastic Order.

24 *Aggregates (khandha)*:

The five groups of material form, feeling, perception, mental formations and consciousness into which the Buddha analyses the living being.

25　Conditioned things refer to phenomenal existence—samsara.

26　*One Bound Upstream:* A Non-returner (anagami).

27　*Recluse (samana):* Here used in the special sense of those who have reached the four supramundane stages.

28　*The Eightfold Path (attangika magga):*
　　Right Understanding, Right Thought, Right Speech, Right Action, Right Livelihood, Right Effort, Right Mindfulness and Right Concentration.
　　Four Noble Truth (catu sacca):
　　suffering, the cause of suffering, the cessation of suffering and the Path leading to the cessation of suffering.

29　*Tathagata:*
　　Truth-bearer. The Buddhas refer themselves as Tathagatas having discovered the Four Noble Truths, the common teaching of all Buddhas.

30　Three courses of action refer to the tenfold good or bad action.

31　The meaning of this injunction is: "Cut down the forest of lust, but do not mortify the body".

32　*Khana:*
　　Opportunity refers to conditions of spiritual progress which the Buddha sasana provides to seekers of Nibbana. There are six such conditions, such as , the advent of the Buddha, One living at that time in the Buddha land, the hearing of the Dhamma, not to be disabled, to be endowed with right understanding, the opportunity to enter the Sangha.

33 *Thirty-six currents of craving:*
   The three cravings—for sensual pleasure, for perpetual existence and for annihilation—in relation to each of the twelve bases—the six sense organs, including mind, and their corresponding objects.

34 To be cut off are the five "lower fetters" of self-illusion, doubt, blind adherence to rites and rituals, lust and ill-will. To be abandoned are the five "higher fetters" of craving for the Brahma divine realms with forms, craving for the formless Brahma divine realms, conceit, restlessness and ignorance. To be cultivated are the five spiritual faculties: faith, energy, mindfulness, concentration and wisdom. The five bonds are greed, hatred, delusion, false views and conceit.

35 Deathless is Nibbana. See note to v. 202.

36 *Holy man (brahmana):*
   Originally Rishis – Sages, men of spiritual stature; by the time of the Buddha the brahmins had become a privileged priesthood, defined in terms of birth and lineage. The Buddha, however, identified the true "holy man" as the Arahat, who merits the term through inward purity and holiness only. The term also applies to those leading a contemplative life dedicated to gaining Arahatship. *Uncreate:* Everything in samsara, being conditioned, is created, formed. Nibbana, being unconditioned is uncreate, beyond formation.

37 *This shore:* Internal sense organs
   Other shore: external sense objects; both: I-ness and my-ness.

38 In the time of the Buddha such ascetic practices as wearing matted hair and garments of hides were considered marks of holiness.

Be A Lamp Upon Yourself
Compilation

The usefulness of this book is in its concise approach to the basic teachings of the Buddha.

I Wonder Why
Ven. Thubten Chodron

This book covers the most fundamental questions and issues that arise in the minds of modern individuals who are new to this tradition of practical spirituality. Written in a clear and engaging language, this book presents the Buddhist approach to the fundamental issues and concerns of daily life.

Working With Anger
Ven. Thubten Chodron

This book describes Buddhist methods for subduing and preventing anger, not by changing what is happening, but by framing it differently.

❀ Other titles published by Kong Meng San Phor Kark See Monastery

Settling Back Into The Moment
Joseph Goldstein

This book is a compilation of excerpts that are words of timeless truths, words that are meant for reflection, words that talk straight to your heart.

Published with kind permission from Sukhi Hotu.

Dhammapada
Ven. Acharya Buddharakkhita

The Dhammapada, which enshrines the spirit of the Buddhas' teachings, is a book for all times, a book to be cherished and loved. May it bring light to your life!

Published with kind permission from Sukhi Hotu.

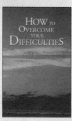

How to Overcome Your Difficulties
Ven. Dr. K. Sri. Dhammananda

Are you worried? Are you miserable? If so, you are invited to read this booklet to develop a better understanding of your problems. It is dedicated to you and to those who worry.

Three Teachings
Ven. Tenzin Palmo

Ven. Tenzin Palmo's Teachings on Retreat, Mahamudra Practice and Mindfulness are a delight to read. Transcribed from talks that she gave in Singapore in May 1999, the teachings are delivered in plain language, seasoned with plenty of audience participation. Each subject is discussed with humour, liveliness and compassion. She has the great gift of showing how the Dharma can be integrated into every aspect of our lives.

Preparing For Death And Helping The Dying
Ven. Sangye Khadro

This booklet answers a genuine need in today's world: to know more about death and how to help dying people. The discomfort we have towards death is because we think it will be a terrible, painful and depressing experience. However, it doesn't have to be so. Dying can be a time of learning and growth; a time of deepening our love, our awareness of what is important in life, and our faith and commitment to spiritual beliefs and practices.

Awakening a Kind Heart
Ven. Sangye Khadro

Everybody wants to be happy and free of problems. The two short teachings in this book explain simply and clearly how we can achieve this happiness by transforming our usual self-cherishing attitude and awakening a kind heart.

The Significance and Benefits of Six-Syllable Mantra Recitation
HE Drubwang Konchok Norbu Rinpoche

Are you curious about the origin of the Six-Syllable mantra? Or what the Four-arm Chenrezig means? Read this book for a better understanding. Based on a series of teachings given by His Eminence Drubwang Konchok Norbu Rinpoche of the Drikung Kagyu lineage, this book also explains the benefits and importance of doing the Mani recitation, and the mental state in which the recitation is to be conducted.

Stories 1-50

Stories 51-100

Tales of the Buddha's Former Lives Stories 51-100

Tales of the Buddha's Former Lives is a collection of simple stories written along the line of Aesop's Fables. Though meant for readers of all ages, they are especially useful to older children and teenagers, as these stories promote and highlight virtuous conduct and good behaviour, especially those human values that contribute to harmony, pleasure and progress.

Transforming Our Daily Activities
Ven. Thubten Chodron

Spiritual practice need not be separated from daily living. Here is a book that teaches you how you can lead a more fulfilling life according to the Buddha's teachings and transform your daily activities into acts of compassion and loving-kindness. You can live and breathe the Dharma even while at work, driving or doing grocery shopping!

Practical Vipassana Meditation Exercises
Ven. Mahasi Sayadaw

Transcribed from a discourse given by the late Ven. Mahasi Sayadaw, this book addressed to lay people describes the subtleties and method of Vipassana meditation practice in a plain, easy and concise language. Showing us the path to liberation through the way of mindfulness, it is not the kind of book that one reads for reading's sake.

* English & Chinese Editions

Discovering Meditation
Ven. Godwin Samararatne

"Forget what you have read and heard. Just be simple, practical and find out. This can be so fascinating; if you can have the openness to learn, you can discover so much. This is meditation. Not taking anything for granted. How grateful we should be that we have this experience. I call it the laboratory of mind and body. So please, generate a fascination for this, develop a curiosity for this. Find this the most meaningful thing one can do in this life, because it is learning all the time about thoughts, about emotions, about perceptions, about so many things in this world of ours." — *Godwin Samararatne*

佛说父母恩重难报经
Filial Piety Sutra

慈鸦尚还哺，羔羊犹跪足，若不尽孝道，何以分人畜？做个孝顺的儿女，当读《佛说父母恩重难报经》，以报亲恩。

* English & Chinese Editions

七月是不是鬼节？
Is The 7th Lunar Month The Ghosts' Season?

七月真的是鬼门关大开、祭拜"好兄弟"的节日吗？
本书告诉您事情的真相……

* English & Chinese Editions

点亮心灯 (汇编)
Be A Lamp Upon Yourself

佛法如灯，照亮心灵的暗室。
智慧如海，冲破心灵的桎梏。

如果有人邀请您走一趟般若之旅，
点一盏心灵之灯，您是否愿意？

开阔心，清净心
Open Heart, Clear Mind
土登却准法师 著　涂炳忠 译

作者以浅白易懂的语言，表达出对佛法的清晰理解，能使一般人，尤其是对佛教还不熟悉的人，了解佛法，运用佛法，并从中获益。

心灵曙光
Basic Buddhism for Beginners
土登却准法师 著　涂炳忠 译

在修学佛法的过程中，我们难免会遇到一些困难与疑问。作者针对一般人的疑问提出了独到的见解，仿佛黎明中的一道曙光，射入读者的心灵，净除内心的困惑，带来智慧的光芒，让有心于修学佛法的朋友，能进一步了解并实践佛陀的教诲。

生死两相安
Preparing for Death and Helping The Dying
桑耶卡卓法师 著　涂炳忠 译

死亡并非一切的结终，而是进入另一世的门槛。
勇于面对死亡，才会勇于活在当下。
只有接受死亡，才能接受人生中的悲欢离合。
希望这本小册子，能让您对死亡有初步的了解，并对如何协助临终者有基础的认识。

告别嗔怒，步向安宁
Working with Anger
土登却准法师 著　涂炳忠 译

佛陀是一位心灵的医疗师，他传授了许多处理情绪与烦恼的实用方法，其中一些对治嗔恚的方法，非常适合运用在日常生活中。只要我们能够掌握这些方法，生活就不再有烦恼！

怎样克服你的困难
How to Overcome Your Difficulties
达摩难陀法师 著

您忧愁苦恼吗？如果您有这种感觉，就请您阅读这本小册子。它能让您对自己的问题有更深入的了解。这本小册子就是献给您和被忧愁所笼罩的人。

地藏菩萨本愿经
白话解释 胡维铨 演述

众生度尽，方证菩提；
地狱不空，誓不成佛。

在地藏经里，释迦牟尼佛宣说地藏菩萨的深重誓愿~累劫勤苦，分身无数，百千方便，利益救拔教化罪苦众生。

唤醒一颗善良的心
Awakening A Kind Heart

桑耶卡卓法师

人人都希望快乐，远离烦恼。本书的两则开示精简扼要地解释如何扭转我们向来的自私心态，以唤醒一颗善良的心，证得快乐、自在。

持诵六字大明咒
的重要性及其利益
The Significance and Benefits of Six-Syllable Mantra Recitation

竹旺贡觉诺布仁波切 著

六字大明咒的起源何在？四臂观音有什么含义？这本小册子收录了直贡噶举派的大成就者竹旺贡觉诺布仁波切的开示，当中解释了持诵六字大明咒的利益及其重要性，与在念诵时应该生起的正确心态。

从佛教角度来探讨
美满婚姻生活
A Happy Married Life

达摩难陀长老 著

宗教能帮你克服问题，只要你懂得如何运用所学过的宗教教义，就能有技巧地避免误会，失望与烦躁问题的产生。与此同时，宗教教义的学习与熟修，也能使我们培育出忍辱与包容体谅。这些优良的性格品质，有助于大家过着幸福美满的婚姻生活……

A Rose for your Pocket
为你别上一朵红玫瑰
Thich Nhat Hanh

All of us are showered with tender love for many years, and without even knowing it, we are quite happy with that. Only when it has vanished do we awaken with a start. This book, dedicated to all mothers, past, present and future, expresses just how dear and precious our own parents are. It tells us truly how our parents are the most wonderful treasures that we are given.

多年以来，我们一直徜徉在温暖的母爱的海洋中，甚至还身在福中不知福，把一切视为是理所当然的。直到瞬间失去了母亲后，我们才恍然醒悟，悔不当初。只可惜，这一切都已经太迟了。此书献给所有过去，现在与未来的母亲们，以表诉我们的父母是如何的可敬与珍贵。它真实地告诉我们，父母是我们被给予最美好的宝藏。

三皈五戒 DVD
3 Refuges & 5 Precepts

What is the Significance of Taking 3 Refuges & 5 Precepts ?

This 40-minute DVD features the very foundations of what it takes to be a Buddhist - Taking Refuge in the Triple Gem and abiding by moral guidelines to sow the seeds of peace and happiness in our everyday life. With coverage of all 3 Buddhist traditions, this is a good introduction for anyone wish to become a Buddhist. Complimentary DVD available in 5 languages (English, Mandarin, Hokkien, Cantonese and Bahasa Indonesia).

* For a detailed list of all the books we published, please visit www.kmspks.org
内容会不时更新，若欲知晓最新的内容，请上网www.kmspks.org查阅。

HOW TO
REACH US

We are at:

Kong Meng San Phor Kark See Monastery
(Bright Hill Temple)
88 Bright Hill Road Singapore 574117

Homepage: http://**www.kmspks.org**

At Bishan Interchange (where Bishan MRT Station is),
take SBS Bus No. 52 & 410 (White Plate).
In less than 10 minutes,
the bus will arrive at the bus-stop right in front
of our temple's front gate.
You won't miss it!

AWAKEN to…

Compassion & Wisdom on the journey of life…

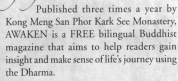

Published three times a year by Kong Meng San Phor Kark See Monastery, AWAKEN is a FREE bilingual Buddhist magazine that aims to help readers gain insight and make sense of life's journey using the Dharma.

Get your free copy from these outlets:

AWARENESS PLACE
光明坊
Blk 231 Bain Street
#01-63 Bras Basah Complex S(180231)

AWARENESS PLACE WELL-BEING CENTRE
艺觉坊
Blk 261 Waterloo Street #01-42
Waterloo Centre S(180261)

SINGAPORE BUDDHIST FEDERATION
新加坡佛教总会
59 Lorong 24A Geylang S(398583)

SINGAPORE BUDDHIST LODGE
新加坡佛教居士林
17 Kim Yam Road S(239329)

TAI PEI BUDDHIST CENTRE
大悲佛教中心
2 Lavender Street S(338823)

CI YAN VEGETARIAN HEALTH FOOD
慈缘轩
8/10 Smith Street S(058917)

* Whilst stocks last

The Dharma Propagation Division in Kong Meng San Phor Kark See Monastery works tirelessly in all areas to benefit all sentient beings. We skilfully bring the Dharma home to each and everyone.

Y.talk

A series of self-enrichment and interactive talks that target to help young professionals to relax, discover Buddhism and its relevance in daily life. A wide range of topics and discussions are conducted by Buddhist and Non- Buddhist Professionals. Other youth programmes include Y.cultivation, Y.care, Y.arts and culture, and Temple Trail. Visit http://youth.kmspks.org/ for more info.

Saturday and Sunday School

Established to sow and nurture the seeds of Buddhahood in our younger generation, it shares the Dharma with the young in a warm, supportive and inspiring environment. Call 6849 5329, visit http://www.kmspks.org/education/ sunschool.htm or e-mail: sundayschool@ kmspks.org to be a Dharma volunteer, or sign up for the school.

Dharma Courses & Activities

Understand what Buddhism really is about. Learn various authentic methods of Buddhist meditation, or realise deep insights through guided retreats by qualified Dharma masters. For these and more, visit http://www.kmspks.org/events and http://www.kmspks.org/events/calendar.htm

Community Development & Training

Community development and training department's mission is to empower individuals and groups of people with knowledge and skills they need to effect change in their own lives and in the community. Training opportunities and materials will be organised where individuals and groups of people can acquire, practise, experience and share skills and knowledge to make life meaningful and fulfilling for themselves and others. Dhammic values and principles are the essence of all the department's programmes. Call 6849 5300 or email community@kmspks.org

TLC Student Care Centre

Looking for a place where your child can learn about the spirit of compassion? Tender Loving Care Student Care Centre nurtures your child's self-esteem, mental attitude and ethical conduct with a modern holistic educational approach. Call 6310 6410, e-mail tlcscc@kmspks.org or visit www.tenderlovingcare.sg to find out more.

SPONSORSHIP FORM

The gift of truth excels all other gifts . . .
The Buddha

If you would like to share the Gift of the Dharma, which is the greatest gift of all, with others by supporting the production cost of Dharma books, CDs and magazines for Free Distribution, kindly photocopy the next page and fill in your particulars. Cheques/money orders should be made payable to **"KMSPKS Monastery"** and sent to:

Kong Meng San Phor Kark See Monastery
Awaken Publishing & Design
88 Bright Hill Road, Singapore 574117

(For overseas readers, please send bankdrafts in Singapore currency. Please include $10 for bank charges.)

** Please note that the monastery is **NOT** able to accept cheques in foreign currency.*

You can also donate online via eNets or Giro at
http://kmspks.org/about/donate
(*Please select 'printing of Dharma Materials'
and type in the donation amount.)

YOUR FEEDBACK MATTERS

*If you have any enquiries
or book, CD & DVD related suggestions,
please call (65)6849 5300 or e-mail: publication@kmspks.org*

Name _____

Highest Educational Level _____

Occupation _____

Address _____

_____

Tel (O)_____(H)_____

(Hp) _____

E-mail _____
(*Would you like to receive our* **Dharma, Music and Prayer Podcast?** ❏ *Yes* ❏ *No*)

Donation: $_____

       ❏ Cash ❏ Cheque No. _____

Do you require an official receipt? ❏ Yes ❏ No

Would you like to receive emails on upcoming talks, retreats or other events of the monastery? ❏ Yes ❏ No

Where did you obtain this book?_____

_____

THE MERITS OF PRODUCING BUDDHIST TEACHINGS AND BUDDHA IMAGES

1. One's light karmic misgivings will dissolve, while heavy ones lighten.

2. One will be protected by devas, and be unharmed by natural and man-made disasters.

3. One will always be free from the suffering of hatred and vengeance.

4. One will be unharmed by yaksas, evil spirits and wild beasts.

5. One's mind will be at peace, free from harm and nightmares.

6. One's complexion will be radiant.

7. One will be full of auspicious energy.

8. One who practises the Dharma wholeheartedly will have adequate living necessities.

9. One's family will be harmonious and be blessed with fortune and wisdom.

10. One who practises what one preaches will be respected and loved by all.

11. One who is dull-minded will gain wisdom.

12. One who is ill will gain health.

13. One who is poor will gain wealth.

14. One will be free of being reborn in the negative realms.

15. One will be able to help others grow in wisdom and gain great merit in doing so.

16. One will always be able to learn the Dharma, till one's wisdom and spiritual penetrations are fully grown and becomes a Buddha.